Damsel in Distress

Georgia Moon

BookLeaf Publishing

Presentation by *BookLeaf Publishing*

Web: www.bookleafpub.com

E-mail: info@bookleafpub.com

ISBN: 9789357213356

First edition 2022

Damsel

You know her as distressed.
Maiden in need of rescue.
Only by beauty, she is blessed.

Where, oh where, is he?
I have searched high and low.
Where could my knight be?

Portray her as defenceless,
Left to the kindness of men.
Let this become consensus.

Omit her bottomless strength,
Story no book could carry.
For survival, she spares no length.

Back scarred with memories,
Pinned by the weight it carries,
Calluses kiss her extremities.

What she has, she has in spite,
Of the forces who seek to take it,
A testament to her fight.

Let us write her a new story,
Our beloved damsel, strong.
Let her take her own glory.
Capable, all along.

Dawn

In the beginning God created man.
Man was given wealth, food, water.
Man was not satisfied.

To answer man, God created woman.
Woman was taken from man
Woman was his helper.

Woman was presented to man.
Man accepted.
They were united in flesh.
Man is satisfied.

Woman is not satisfied.
The forbidden fruit,
Eat it and you shall die.
Could this be deception?
Does she mind?

To answer woman, God condemns:
With pain shall you birth your children
Your husband, you will serve
This is your punishment.
This is your purpose.

Daughter

Dear daughter,

Two lines mark my induction
Into this class of women, elite.
Positive, so they tell me.
Positive, I repeat.

Dear daughter,

It's not that I don't care for you,
Some way I feel I do.
It's that I am not sure I yield,
The things I am expected to.

I'm not like other ladies,
Saintly and mild and clean.
Like Joanna often wondering,
Have I ever seen them bleed?

I am late, I am messy
All the things they revile.
I am fat, I am lazy
Unable to reconcile.

Dear daughter,

My time is up,
My mind unclear.
Tell me this is right
I have wronged you, I fear.

Dear daughter,

My growing little artichoke,
They say you can finally hear.
Finally the chance to tell you,
I'm glad you are here.

Yes I am frightened,
Of failing in everything I do.
I worry for the ramifications
That may have on you.

I worry that I might drop you.
Or ignore your cries in the night.
Or that you might be born ugly
Make the nurse gasp in fright.

Now I can admit this
For this much I know is true,
Scared as I may be
I am excited to get to know you.

Dear daughter,

Ringing. Countless. Endless.
Voices of people without faces.

These are your people,
The ones who will hold your hand.
Today I told your family,
22 weeks 'fore you land.

Giddy so the seem,
Smiles litter their faces.
Caution I must heed,
Deception hides in unlikely places.

Dear daughter,

"Support" is what they preach
Poison is what they spit.
My time with you now clouded
With shame I cannot admit.

Rules forever my enemy
The line too heavy to tow,
Many directions I am pulled
Yet, have nowhere to go.

Sit often
Raised foot is best
But not too often
Perfect women don't rest.

Eat many greens
Raw fish do not touch
Avoid soft cheese
For caffeine you will lust.

Stop your daily working,
Home is where you must be.
Be sure to make money,
Support you child's every need.

Doomed I am to fail,
I will give my all, I vow.
A good mother has been promised,
I will learn how.

Dear daughter,

Each day I feel your strength,
Marvel as you grow.
Each centimetre demanding
Another piece of me go.

I am a shell of who I was,
Fractured, broken and bruised.
At a time I am to be sure,
I have never been more confused.

Dear daughter,

Now the days grow colder,
The sun has turned to snow.
I know you will soon be with me,
I wonder, will I ever glow?

I know I have been knighted,
To motherhood I am bound.
Yet I feel little connection,
Am I letting you down?

You are my daughter,
This much I know is true.
No matter what life throws at us,
You will find me beside you.

I long to hear your voice,
See a smile swallow your cheek,
To learn how each little piece
Makes you unique.

I will that feeling to come.
Every hour of every day.
I really want to love you,
For this, I pray.

Delivery

Was it natural?
Could you feel every pain?
Did you enjoy it?
Didn't once complain?

Did you risk your body?
Put your life on the line?
Only two hours?
Much less than mine.

Would you do it all again?
Thank God for his gift?
Do you know you are lucky?
Feel your life shift?

Did you do it in a bath?
At home in bed?
You did it in a hospital?
I'd rather be dead.

To be a woman,
This task has been set.
Agony is measurable,
Who will suffer best?

Dextrose

Sweetness.
Sugared and spiced.
Nice -

Lady.
Proper and prim.
Kind-

Spirited.
Calming and wise.
Soft -

Spoken.
Tender and mild.
Nurturing -

Mother.
Smiling and fair.
Weak -

Willed.
Submissive and scared.
Blind -

Faith.
Never fight.
Never dare.

That's what little girls are shaped on.

Disclaimer

I dreamed of having a daughter,
Of holding you in my arms.
In my mind saw pictures,
Ballerina perched on stairs.

I saw us in the bathroom
Before the school bell's song.
Brushing tangles out of hair,
Laughing each second on.

In my mind you were always happy,
Skipping, never walk.
Danced at every intersection,
Sung at every stop.

Pink was your colour,
In your nursery it showed.
Butterflies in ever corner,
On every hanger, a gown.

Before I ever met you,
I had assumed what you would be.
Forced you to fit the mould,
Another victim of society.

Written in your code it lay,
The mark of your demise,
A code made entirely of X,
No freedom found in Y.

Less before you could do more,
Explains a thing or two.
Over 130 million still missing
Girls, just like you.

For those who evade destruction,
Embryo permitted to form.
The fight continues still.
Form every dusk to every dawn.

Branded by temptation,
For this you will be punished.
Taught to conceal your anatomy,
Shame is your first language.

Legs crossed never opened,
Comfort is not a question.
Beauty is pain, repeated.
Good girls don't fight it.

Punished for falling victim,
The cross you are forced bear.
Break match before flame is lit.
Your future, my gift.

I'm sorry my daughter,
If it were me who willed it so.
Many smiles will be dishonest.
For into woman, you will grow.

Dichotomy

Arm him from conception,
Gift him toys of sword and steel.
Heroes proficient with violence,
Cape to symbolise beau idéal.

Enrol him into sports,
Injury becomes expectation.
Where contact is urged.
Intimidation as per instruction.

Fights among his friends,
"Boys will be boys"
Conversation viewed as weakness,
Expression marked as noise.

Strip girls of these defences,
Discouraged from confrontation.
Teach them elegance and poise,
To fulfill their expectations.

Force them to walk as peers,
Exist in perfect harmony.
Boys bred to fight,
Fear is female reality.

Doctrine

In the name of the father,
I commend my faith,
Loyal servant in heart and deed.

In the name of the father,
I renounce all sin,
Perform penance when I do not succeed.

In the name of the father,
I commit to service,
Learn to tend to His every need.

In the name of the father,
I accept second place,
Power is not given to 'she'.

In the name of the father,
I learn to be silent,
Speak only when someone has spoken to me.

We are all born in his image,
Such is what we preach.
A life of service rewarded with salvation,
Such is what we teach.

Before our girls can vote,
They can recite this passage, three

In the name of the father,
I submit to you.

And of the Son,
I am lesser than you.

And of the Holy Spirt,
I exist to please.

Deliberate

There once was a farmer,
Walked a lone path each light.
From house to field,
Grain tickling at his sides.

He had a wife
Bound when grain was seed,
Family became her riches,
A son soon to be.

The farmer became teacher,
Sharing his great touch.
Soon two hands tended the garden
Two hands, twice as much.

Each day the son grew taller,
The father turning grey.
Another was in order,
What price shall we pay?

Together they ventured,
Deep into the city's aisles.
Found newspaper held a promise,
The number hastily, was dialled.

Father answered hence,
The negotiations began.
Many hours they deliberated,
Man to fellow man.

After the talking was through,
The price was sealed in shake.
Twelve goats for his great prize.
Twelve goats would seal her fate.

Without her being asked,
She was escorted to the altar
Her eyes danced along the floor,
Not for a second, would she falter.

This is what she was born for.
A daughter, into one future bred.
The price for her hand in partnership,
Greater than that of her head.

Date

I approach him,
Slowly,
Buckling under the weight of his stare.
Unblinking thus,
I fumble my eyes,
Unknowing where to lay them.
Does the walk ever end?

Church
Bells in the background,
Fingers dance over keys,
Veil forcing head into bow,
Flowers masking tremor,
Make-up masking terror,
The priest calls.

Dinner
Ambience set by candlelight,
I am searching for my seat.
Scanning photos in place of GPS.
Is he standing patiently?
Hands clasped tightly.
Is he standing?
Has he stood?

Church
A thousand eyes cast upon me,
Beads of sweat start to form.
A promise so unreachable,
Surely they must know.
Does he sense my words are empty?
Perhaps I am,
Unjustly so.

Dinner
In this room there is only one other
Soul, lone as mine.
Glued to his watch,
It is clear he is expecting.
Common purpose,
Yet his face lies.

Church
Breathe, try to enjoy it.
Today you have dreamed of.
The day you become woman.
A family girl.
A home.

Dinner
Too late now, he has seen me.
Though I am searching still.
Deep in his eyes a man is buried,
"Sorry, I didn't recognise you."

"It's an old photo. Bill"

Church
With this ring,
The deed will be done.
In parent's eye, a shimmer.
Their darling girl, has won.

Dinner
As he leaves he carries hope with him,
My purpose, unfilled.
Worth equal to Happily Ever After.
This failure, like my womanhood.
Destined for disaster.

Daisy

Blown lame in the wind,
Daisies rarely stand alone.
Linked in chain is she.

Desire

Growing into herself,
She loses what she had.
Once bound to gentility,
She knew softness and care.
Now with each step,
Becoming less than human.

Worth quantified,
Seen in length of skirt.
Stares stained with opinion.
Nameless, faceless. Body -
Strip her of her story
Cover from head to toe.

Consequential non-compliance,
With each fabric-inch, diminish.
Slaughter in criticism,
Parts of her person buried.
She is object to be beholden,
Illusion dressed as will.

Beyond fabric, her body
Belonging not to her.
Subject to outside approval,
Shape contorting to mould.

Conditional acceptance.
Each comment more real.

Poisoned with negativity,
The mind transforms.
Mirror branded with hate,
Reflected in self-image.
Inner monologue to match,
Alleged social norms.

Seed has been planted,
With society, she believes lesser.
Injustice easier to swallow,
Resistance becoming scarcer.
Name carried off in wind,
Replaced with slur and slander.

Use her to your will
Posing limb against her body.
Flaunt her in your movies,
See her on every poster.
Silence where protest once stood.
A vessel to male desire.

Diabolos

First is he who is prideful,
Conqueror in mind and deed.
War is his legacy.
A soldier astute and proud.

No matter the cost, vanquish.
No matter the deed, do.
Forever, she is branded victim.
A trophy, glistens in his eye.

Second is he who is greedy,
His want taking precedence.
Consent is not in question,
The ends justify the means.

If you want it take it,
Settle for nothing less.
Never-mind the damage done.
Never-mind the consequence.

Third is he named glutton,
Excess is your vice.
Driven to drown in desire
Satisfaction, a myth.

And when she starts to question,
A yes rolling into no,
Unable to stop once started.
How can society expect it so?

Fourth is he who is envious,
Jealous of what others have.
Her attention ever changing.
You will take it back.

It was her fault for wandering,
Leaving the family home.
What you did you had to do,
Reclaimed your right by vow.

Fifth is he named sloth,
Unruled by the concept of earn,
What is his, believed given.
In practice, it is taken.

Unresponsive equal to permission,
Incapacity marks opportunity.
No fist nor fight nor tears.
Effort conditional to innocence.

Sixth is he who is angry,
Punishment is his game.
Determined to cause suffering,
Soothed only by pain.

Born female, doomed to hate
Targeted for being 'she'.
This one knows of his action
And does it all the same.

Seventh is he who is lustful,
Drunk with pleasure gained.
Flesh is what the feats on,
Desire clouds his brain.

Her wants inconsequential,
Pleasure can be one-sided.
Submission is her destiny,
Will? Consider it broken.

Seven of our most deadly,
Sins surmounting to evil.
It takes only one to commit them.
One.

One in six.

Dialogue

Her silence fills the room,
Dialogue ripe with injustice.
She holds her tongue.

Prejudicial jury,
Criminalise the victim.
She holds her tongue.

Guilty until proven honest,
Evidence circumstantial.
She holds her tongue.

Words weightless,
'No' misheard as yes.
She holds her tongue.

Statement turned interrogation,
Memories blur.
She holds her tongue.

Forever branded broken,
Relationships shift.
She holds her tongue.

Behaviour drew target,
Guilt held in fist.
She holds her tongue.

Shame in place of mourning,
Fault hard to place.
She holds her tongue.

Threats of further violence,
Unable to escape.
She holds her tongue.

Deviant

Female led fatality -
Hollywood's favourite bandit.
Lipstick sealed brutality,
Her arrival, not as you'd planned it.

Cast in deep shadow,
Silhouette defiantly shines.
Lace-laden window.
Her soul as black as night.

Weaponising question,
Motive cannot be guessed.
Anticipating action?
Better odds with chess.

Theft undetected,
Power she 'cannot' hold.
Comfort ill-affected,
Anxiety highlighted, bold.

Diagnosis

Enter, hands clasped
Bleach stung nose.
Avoid gaze, validate,
Your attendance.
And nothing more.
Time, with fear, grows.
Your name is called.
List each symptom, gravity too great for the weight of words.
Under microscope before hands have left desk.
Encompassing.
Inescapable. His gaze says so much, you wonder, has he heard?
Tongue runs over teeth, sigh clouds the room. Are you certain?
Question - Deception, a sin. Suffering a contest you will not win.
Measure, stick to the facts. Aid his agenda, notice Dr on his back.
Sure-footed he reaches his conclusion. No poke or prod in sight.
I see this problem often,
Common in girls your age.
Hormonal fluctuations.
It's only your period.
Approaching the change.
You're likely anxious
- Insert text here -

Digital

Upload successful.

How long before first like?
Might I beat the record?
Which friend first in line?
How many comments will follow?
Popularity numerised.
Will people be impressed?
Positive opinion, will I find?

Will mum leave me a comment?
Embarrassing like the last?
Is this a flattering angle?
Surpassing uploads past?
Will my crush see this?
Leave a comment, how fast?

New comments.

Why are you so fat?
You look like such a cow.
Body flat as ironing board.
If you were my daughter, wow.
You're totally asking for it.
This can't be allowed.

Ugliest dog I've seen,
Sorry but you've gained weight.
Your body is so misshapen.
Ashamed to be your date.
Definitely a hussy.
Fake.

Dysphoria

Pose as diversity,
Bred into conformity.
Into triangle turned sphere,
Destiny planned, clear.

Into pink thrust girls,
Skirts and dress to follow.
Doll every occasion,
Ballerina your allocation.

Cursed to disconnection,
Smile to hide the pain.
Lie encrypted in biology,
At war with psychology.

Long for brothers' freedom,
To roll and play in mud.
Body to match identity,
Mere thought, obscenity.

Fight to keep it hidden,
You are bound to untruth.
Compliance your protection,
Persecution following detection.

Discrepancy

77 cents to every man's dollar,
Equal labour expected.
Reward not with promotion,
Sensitivity viewed as unfitness.

To work is a privilege,
For many who will search.
Myriad of Industries un-yielding,
Interview scarce to find.

Candidacy privilege still,
For girls whose education denied,
Each step the men have taken,
She is many behind.

Defiance

Biology gives you privilege.
No mask nor wall in sight.
Dominance sealed in DNA.
Submission yours, by right.
Allegedly.

You see her on the surface,
Unphased to look beneath.
Desire softens your reflexes.
Your movements, predictable.
Meek.

The mould your kind has built,
Some will surely follow.
Expectation of legacy,
Immortality.
Tomorrow.

With each decade's dawn,
The wind has been changing.
Circumstance forced rebellion,
A new future,
Emerging.

In men's absence, survived.
Became mother, wife and winner.
Proficient in his tools,
Supporting the family she raised.
Un-ruled.

Independence proved in sweat,
Careers came to be.
Women inspired by self-worth,
Rich with sufficiency.
The fight does not end.
Continuing.

Along with work came voice,
Time for them to shout.
As they had before, they fought,
For the rights,
Their rights,
To count.

Suffering birthed suffrage,
Proof of a worthy fight.
Evidence of the spirit within
Yearning for freedom.
Burning,
Bright.

Some were born with privilege,
Others in how they were raised,

Cheap are the rights that are given,
Strong are the ones we've made.

Do

Next time she passes by you,
Trailed by strange men,
Don't see,
Do.

Next time your mates whistle,
Joke as she walks by,
Don't see,
Do.

Next time they pay her less,
When you have done no more,
Don't see,
Do.

Next time she is called deserving,
For her outfit choices that day,
Don't see,
Do.

Next time she is shamed,
For being unmarried at any age,
Don't see,
Do.

Next time she is labelled hussy,
For wanting things same as you,
Don't see,
Do.

Next time her pain is invalidated,
Called weak for being she,
Don't see,
Do.

Next time she is given looks,
For feeding children where she please,
Don't see,
Do.

Next time she is considered less than,
For mothering isn't her call,
Don't see,
Do.

Next time she is branded improper,
For choosing comfort over grace,
Don't see,
Do.

Equality lies with you.

www.ingramcontent.com/pod-product-compliance
Lightning Source LLC
Chambersburg PA
CBHW051746130826
49812CB00033B/1020
* 9 7 8 9 3 5 7 2 1 3 3 5 6 *